THE
COMPANY
YOU
KEEP

THE
COMPANY
YOU
KEEP

WHAT YOUR BROKER WON'T TELL YOU
ABOUT EXITING YOUR BUSINESS

DAVE ARENS, RUSSELL SAMPLES
& TIMOTHY KNEEN

Advantage®

Published by Advantage, Charleston, South Carolina.
Member of Advantage Media Group.

ADVANTAGE is a registered trademark, and the Advantage colophon is a trademark of Advantage Media Group, Inc.

Printed in the United States of America.

10   9   8   7   6   5   4   3   2   1

ISBN: 978-1-64225-406-8
LCCN: 2022909125

Cover design by Mary Hamilton.
Layout design by Wesley Strickland.

Advantage Media Group is proud to be a part of the Tree Neutral® program. Tree Neutral offsets the number of trees consumed in the production and printing of this book by taking proactive steps such as planting trees in direct proportion to the number of trees used to print books. To learn more about Tree Neutral, please visit **www.treeneutral.com**.

Advantage Media Group is a publisher of business, self-improvement, and professional development books and online learning. We help entrepreneurs, business leaders, and professionals share their Stories, Passion, and Knowledge to help others Learn & Grow. Do you have a manuscript or book idea that you would like us to consider for publishing? Please visit **advantagefamily.com** or call **1.866.775.1696**.

CONTENTS

CHAPTER ONE: 1
YOU ARE HERE

CHAPTER TWO: 19
WHAT YOU MAY HAVE MISSED

CHAPTER THREE: 31
YOU HAVE OPTIONS

CHAPTER FOUR: 49
WHEN SELLING IS THE RIGHT DECISION

CONCLUSION. 61

WHAT MAKES US DIFFERENT 65

CHAPTER ONE:

YOU ARE HERE

As asset managers, wealth managers, and business owners ourselves, we've met with and advised countless entrepreneurs and executives. These conversations have led us to one key conclusion: 85 percent of the businesses that have been sold shouldn't have been sold.

That's a statistic that should make every business owner pay attention because it illustrates the truth that so many really smart businesspeople may have spent years—even generations—building up a successful venture without dedicating even a fraction of that time to creating a succession plan. And then one day they decide that they've had enough. Maybe they're ready to retire. Maybe the family member who they thought would take over isn't interested. Maybe sales are lagging. Maybe sales are booming, and they're struggling to keep up.

Whatever the reason—and we've heard them all—they wake up one morning and recognize that they don't want to run this business anymore. And if they're like many owners, they place a call to an investment banker or a business broker, who advises them to sell without any consideration of other options!

For some businesses, that decision to sell is the correct one. But for most of them, it's not. There's a better way.

This book is the result of that conviction: for most businesses, there are other options that are often far more attractive than simply selling the company. There are other solutions that will help you achieve your goals—solutions that may be more financially lucrative and more emotionally satisfying.

If you believe that the only logical way to exit a business is to sell it to someone else, if you are tired and don't see other options but to sell, we encourage you to stop and read this book.

As a business owner, you have created enormous value. One way to measure that value is in dollars and cents. You can determine the value of your company by what an interested third party offers to pay you.

But there's another way to assess the value of this business you have built. You can measure its value in the differences you have made in hundreds—possibly thousands—of lives, the lives of all the people who have a relationship to your business. The employees and their families, the vendors and experts you have hired, and of course your customers.

The purpose of this book is not to talk you out of selling your company but to talk you into pausing and taking the time to thoroughly explore your options. It's to encourage you to prepare for what comes next. It's to urge you to look beyond the metrics and the numbers, to value your company using more than simply the price someone else is willing to pay for it. Above all, it is to commit to going through a formal planning process to discover how to optimally accomplish all your goals before deciding to sell.

If you're saying right now, "I have thought about it. In fact, I haven't stopped thinking about it for years," you're not alone. We have heard these exact words from others. We can't promise you that we will find a solution that you didn't know about, but we can tell you that we have helped our clients discover better solutions over and over again. Perhaps more importantly, we can promise you that the business brokers and bankers won't be asking you to look for other solutions. If selling the business is really the best answer for you that emerges from our process, you will have more confidence—and more peace—about that decision. If it's not the best answer, we will have developed ideas that may save you a lifetime of work and millions of dollars.

Who We Are

We understand where you are because we have been there. We are business consultants who are also business owners.

Timothy Kneen is an expert at creating growth strategies, performing merger and acquisition work, and executing business best practices. He has started seven companies, taken a company public, and sold other companies to both synergistic and financial buyers. Tim has been a successful real estate developer as well as an owner of businesses in industries as diverse as technology, manufacturing, golf, and fashion. This experience equips him with a unique understanding (that we call real-life experience) of how owners can best grow their companies, when (and if) owners should seek monetization of their life's work, and how to effectively manage the transition of wealth to the next generation.

Russell Samples is a strategic thinker whose career has focused on creating and implementing wealth management solutions for high-net-worth clients and their families. As both a business owner and a fiduciary advisor, Rusty has deep knowledge and skills in trust and estate planning, investment management, wealth transition, and business succession planning. Rusty's knowledge of how to optimize after-tax results for business owners is born from his own family's exposure as business owners.

David Arens has spent close to three decades working with business owners, entrepreneurs, executives, and health professionals as a banker and a fiduciary expert, sharing strategic recommendations that have equipped them to make smarter decisions about how to launch, grow, and exit their businesses while ensuring that their goals are met at each stage of the process. As both an advisor and a business owner, Dave is especially skilled at planning, which is what we believe most business owners are failing at as the first-step approach to selling their companies.

These backgrounds have equipped us with unique expertise. We've owned businesses and have sold even more of them. Some we sold as young owners and now recognize a potential we hadn't seen at the time. We've started many other businesses and, when we were ready, transitioned away from their day-to-day management while still accomplishing the financial rewards we were seeking. We can recommend strategies to do this effectively because we have done it ourselves.

In this book we'll share what's worked as well as any mistakes we've made along the way. Collectively we have more than a hundred years of experience as business owners and business consultants. We've advised CEOs and entrepreneurs in many industries and have developed a proven plan to ensure that your business will live on long after you leave it. Our goal is to equip you with an understanding of the best way to transition from your business and the tools to implement that transition in a logical and strategic way.

A good business consultant is not interested in giving you a sales pitch. We want to have a conversation. We'll ask the questions you'll need to consider, questions that will help you honestly assess the next steps that make sense for you and your business. Questions like: Is there a more efficient way to lower your workload—and your risk? How will you replace the income and benefits you receive from your business? What are the tax implications if you choose to sell? What are your goals for this transition—for yourself, your family, and your key employees who helped you build? What's the target liquidity or risk reduction you are seeking? Would you be willing to own if you can monetize 60 percent of the value? How do you want to reward key stakeholders?

These are challenging questions, but in this book we'll guide you through the steps of asking and answering them to fully understand the implications of any decisions you make. We know how hard it is to create a business and invest in its growth. We also know what happens after you sell. And we're ready to share that knowledge with you.

How You Got Here

It's helpful to get started with a bit of orientation. Think of it as the "You Are Here" spot on a map. Like all the business owners with whom we've worked, we are willing to bet that you've been very successful at building your business. But then you reach a moment where you recognize that your role in the business needs to change.

"I'm exhausted."

"I've missed out on too much of my family's life."

"I'm ready for a new challenge."

"I can't work forever."

"My son/daughter/brother/sister is not interested in taking over."

"The company is struggling, and I'm short on answers."

"The competition is too intense."

Sound familiar? We've heard these and similar statements from many clients. Heck, we have felt them ourselves, and we understand the emotions that have inspired them.

But for too many people, these statements point to only one decision: to sell. Our response is not that selling is bad. There are situations in which it is the correct response to your goals and your business environment. But in all cases, it's critical to evaluate every option available to you—and there are many—before committing to a sales agreement.

Let's take a moment and consider that first statement: "I'm exhausted." Why do owners of great businesses get tired? It's possible that you're focusing so much on the problems you need to fix that you've lost sight of the lives that you are changing. You may struggle with delegating, convinced that no one else can do what you're doing nearly as well. You may have forgotten to be a leader because you're too busy

> **It's critical to evaluate every option available to you—and there are many—before committing to a sales agreement.**

being an administrator. You may not know how you will get to the light at the end of the tunnel.

When you are having these types of emotions, it's easy to jump to a conclusion. We just want you to slow down.

The Five *P*s

We're big believers in encouraging our clients to focus on the message of what we call "the five *P*s." It's a simple statement: proper planning prevents poor processes.

As you've built your business, you've adapted to changing markets, evolving supply chains, and shifting customer needs. But the same proper planning is needed throughout all facets of your business's life cycle, including succession planning/monetization.

It's unfortunate that, too often, this succession planning is ignored or overlooked until you reach a critical point. But those are the very moments when it's the most challenging to pause and carefully assess your options.

We've seen it often: once you decide to sell, that decision can consume you. Our recommendation? Slow down. Honestly consider your response to the question, Why do you want to sell?

The statements we've listed earlier are the most common responses. But too often they're a result of emotion rather than strategic thinking.

For every one of those statements, there's an alternative solution. There's a different strategy that could be implemented, a way to address what's motivating your exit from the business while enabling you to continue to reap the rewards of owning a thriving and successful venture.

It's extremely challenging to build a great business. According to data from the Bureau of Labor Statistics, 20 percent of new businesses fail within their first year, and 50 percent will fail within the first five years of operation. By the end of a decade, only 30 percent of businesses remain. That's a 70 percent failure rate.[1]

If you've beaten these odds, you don't want to just run for the exit when you're ready to step back from the day-to-day management of your business. You must craft a strategy that accomplishes your goals purposefully and thoughtfully.

How do you do this? Let's start with this simple recommendation: *don't hire an investment banker or a business broker.*

---

1   Timothy Carter, "The True Failure Rate of Small Businesses," *Entrepreneur*, January 30, 2021, https://www.entrepreneur.com/article/361350.

Instead we suggest that you hire a business planner, a consultant who can help you identify your key objectives and then assess the options that will enable you to meet those goals. You want a strategist who can guide you through the best steps to take—and when to take them. You may discover that you can make more money and solve your other issues by continuing to own the business rather than selling it.

The best time to have these conversations is before the actual decision to sell needs to be made. Many business owners believe that they're too busy to focus on succession planning. Others have casual conversations about the future of their business but don't engage in serious planning and preparation. We seem to meet a lot of business owners whose decision to sell has been building steadily; a recent event is the trigger that causes them to want to move forward—and to do it now!

Finding the Light

As we reflect on the businesses we've sold and those we've successfully transitioned away from, we can clearly see instances where we'd like a do-over. Tim likes to say, "The inexperience of youth has given way to the experience of wrinkles." In some of our first ventures as business owners, we chose to sell because we hadn't stopped to think about a long-term plan. The short-term money looked very good! We didn't pause to think about what the business could be worth or the people we could help. We didn't take our time. We didn't work with an expert to help us navigate and plan in a way that would enable us to continue on and do what we wanted to do.

We talk about the importance of finding the light at the end of the tunnel—of truly assessing the value of the business you've built and finding solutions to the problems that may be distracting you from what is special and unique about what you've accomplished. Tim has a story that's worth sharing here, demonstrating the importance of stepping back and considering a key question: What else will you do that makes the same money and uses your talents in the same way?

Tim is the partial owner of a search engine optimization company based in Europe. It's a family business, and Tim's nephew is leading it. The company makes $12 million to $15 million a year, and Tim and the other owners were recently offered $50 million to sell the company. Tim's nephew had become frustrated with managing the business and felt it was time to move on.

$50 million. That's a huge sum. That's life-changing money. But they said no.

Why? Because they paused and asked themselves that question: What else can we do that will generate

$12 million to $15 million a year, that we can run part time because of the great team that we've put in place? What could possibly be better than that?

That's the emotional gut-check part of assessing your options when considering a sale. But there's more. It's easy to get caught up in the excitement of a big-dollar offer for a company you've created, but it's critical to make sure that you're fully informed of precisely how a sale might impact you financially. Tim's family did that due diligence. They recognized that after paying the taxes and brokers' fees, $50 million would be reduced to about $25 million. Still a significant sum, but remember, they're operating a business that generates $12 million to $15 million a year. That's far more income than what the $25 million will provide.

Are There Good Reasons to Sell?

Business brokers have a conflict of interest when it comes to your business. They make money when they sell it. It's not surprising that their solution to whatever you're seeking will be to recommend that you sell.

That doesn't mean that it's never the correct decision to sell. When a client discusses their motivations for exiting a business, there are what we view as "okay" reasons to sell. Here are some of those "okay" reasons we hear from our clients:

"There are lots of other high-value transactions going on in our industry, and we should take advantage of the opportunity to exit."

"We've had a big run. We should sell at the highest value."

"If we sell now, all my family's financial goals are accomplished."

All these three reasons require the kind of thoughtful assessment and preparation that we're recommending. You'll want to be certain that the market actually supports the conclusions you've reached. You want to know that now is likely the moment when you can sell the business at its highest value. And you want to clearly understand the financial implications of the sale to confirm that you will indeed accomplish your financial goals. All this, as Dave says, "takes good planning."

Business brokers have a conflict of interest when it comes to your business.

We've briefly touched on the wrong reasons to sell. We've listed the okay reasons. That leaves one category, the good reasons to sell.

In fact, there's really only one:

"There are better people to take this company to the next level."

When that happens, when you've assessed your options and truly understand that a change of ownership will enable your business to continue to excel and succeed, a sale can enable you to pass the leadership role on to someone else. If your goal is to make sure that the business advances, and you know that another owner is the right leader for that advancement, then the sale will support your goal.

As you can see, we're not saying, "Never sell your business." We are saying that there may be other ways to accomplish your goals other than an outright simple sale to a third party.

In the next few chapters, we'll share our collective experience to equip you to make an informed decision about what's next for you and your business. We'll guide you through the strategic decision-making process we use for ourselves and our clients. We'll explore options that you may not have considered and coach you in how best to leverage those options to support your objectives.

We'll ask the questions you need to ask. And if the answers to those questions reveal that it is, in fact, the right time to sell, we'll share our process to help you successfully navigate your exit at far less cost and with far more tax efficiency.

You started your business with a plan. You've grown the business with a clear focus on your goals. The same planning, the same goal orientation, is every bit as important as you decide how to exit the business.

CHAPTER TWO:

WHAT YOU MAY HAVE MISSED

Kelly is an entrepreneur who built a successful small business, one that had $20 million in sales, of which $4.5 million was profit. Kelly was proud of what she accomplished in this entrepreneurial venture, but after fifteen years of twelve-hour days, she was ready for a change. She wanted to focus on a Christian ministry that was important to her. She also wanted to travel and spend more time with her grandchildren, who lived on the other side of the country.

Kelly also recognized that she had grown the company as far as she could. The customer base was shifting, and she knew that someone with fresh ideas

DAVE ARENS, RUSSELL SAMPLES & TIMOTHY KNEEN

and energy would be better equipped to ensure that her company continued to thrive and expand.

Fortunately, there was a strong market for her business. There were several large corporations acquiring smaller companies in her sector.

But before Kelly agreed to the sale, she came to us. There was one factor that made her uncomfortable about selling to a third party. She had twenty-six loyal employees, all of whom had worked hard to help her build the business over fifteen years. She wanted to make sure that those employees were taken care of after her exit.

Kelly asked us to negotiate with the buyer, requesting long-term contracts and equity in the business for all twenty-six of those employees. The buyer wasn't interested—they didn't know these employees and were not willing to cede that much equity to anyone else.

Kelly had thought that there were only two options: continue to run her business or sell it to a third party. But what she had missed was a different strategy—a way to honor her intent to reward her employees for their contributions while enabling her to fulfill her dream for what was next in her life. We recommended a *management-led recap*, in which Kelly could restructure the debt and equity in her company to reduce her personal financial risk by reducing her percentage ownership of the business.

We proposed this because we had spent time with Kelly asking key questions, the biggest of which was, Why do you want to sell your business? Through those conversations, through listening carefully to how Kelly responded, we understood that her decision to sell stemmed from two goals: extract money from the business to support her plans for ministry and travel and de-risk her life to protect her assets. We also knew that Kelly was concerned that her exit would negatively impact her employees.

Our solution was to work with a group of senior employees at Kelly's company who desperately wanted to buy the company but didn't have the resources to match the price offered by that corporate giant. We helped them secure a bank loan for 50 percent of the sales price Kelly had been offered, which was more than enough to allow Kelly to move ahead with what she wanted to do next. The plan was for her to slowly sell the remaining 50 percent of the business to this group of employees over a period of several years. In the meantime, because of her remaining stake in the company, she could receive about $2 million a year in income.

Planning, however, showed us that we could improve on this idea. If Kelly sold 50 percent of a business making $4.5 million at 6x, the total value of the company would be $27 million. So 50 percent is $13.5 million on which she would need to pay taxes. Since Kelly lives in the Midwest, her state tax is 7 percent, and she was in the highest federal bracket, which at the time was 38 percent (45 percent total). In short her tax bill would have been over $6 million.

However, we noted that Kelly had a charitable intent. We suggested moving 25 percent of the equity in her company to a little-known charitable structure called a *charitable support organization*, which allows an active company to be held inside a charitable entity. At her age this created a deduction for a charitable gift of $6.75 million at 45 percent of that gift or $3.03 million. It also reduced the gain on the sale of $6.75 million, so the tax burden dropped to $3.03 million. In short, we crossed the tax burden of selling with the charitable deduction. However, the best part is that we created a known funding source for Kelly's charitable goals.

It's a more tax-efficient strategy. It's a more elegant solution. And it enables Kelly to meet her goals, honor her employees' contribution to her success, and know that a strong team is in place to continue to grow the company.

Most business brokers/bankers would have simply told Kelly to sell. The net result would have been less money for charity, less money for Kelly, diminished or no rewards for the employees who had helped build the business, and unknown change that comes with every buyer. In our solution, Kelly knew that the culture would stay in place. She could be confident in what came next for all the lives her company affected. As she said, "This is just perfect!"

Senior Management - Lead Recap

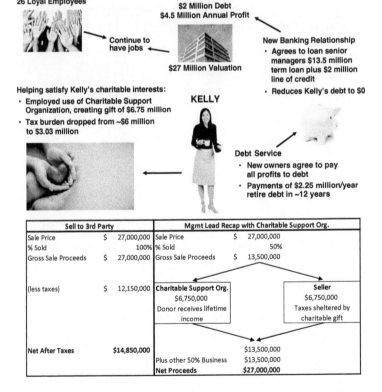

Sell to 3rd Party			Mgmt Lead Recap with Charitable Support Org.		
Sale Price	$	27,000,000	Sale Price	$	27,000,000
% Sold		100%	% Sold		50%
Gross Sale Proceeds	$	27,000,000	Gross Sale Proceeds	$	13,500,000
(less taxes)	$	12,150,000	**Charitable Support Org.** $6,750,000 Donor receives lifetime income		**Seller** $6,750,000 Taxes sheltered by charitable gift
Net After Taxes	$14,850,000			$13,500,000	
			Plus other 50% Business	$13,500,000	
			Net Proceeds	**$27,000,000**	

Kelly, Inc.
$20 Million Sales
$2 Million Debt
$4.5 Million Annual Profit

26 Loyal Employees

Continue to have jobs

$27 Million Valuation

New Banking Relationship
· Agrees to loan senior managers $13.5 million term loan plus $2 million line of credit
· Reduces Kelly's debt to $0

Helping satisfy Kelly's charitable interests:
· Employed use of Charitable Support Organization, creating gift of $6.75 million
· Tax burden dropped from ~$6 million to $3.03 million

KELLY

Debt Service
· New owners agree to pay all profits to debt
· Payments of $2.25 million/year retire debt in ~12 years

Seller's Remorse

Owners don't choose to sell a business on a whim or simply because of a multimillion-dollar offer. There are other factors at work, motivations that may be shaped by financial or emotional issues and concerns.

Yet there is one constant: when they begin to think—really think—through the implications of selling the business, they experience regrets. Those regrets look like this: How am I going to take care of the people who helped me build this business? Will the new owner take care of them or fire them? Will the new owner honor the promises I've made? How will they treat my customers? Will they destroy the brand name I've spent years building? How will I explain this to my key customers? What if the buyer runs this into the ground? I still live in this community! Are my financials in proper order?

It's a difficult dilemma, the conflict between knowing that you're ready to exit and worrying about what will happen when you're gone. But too many owners think that there's only one path—the path of selling.

When we encourage them to pause, to think, when we ask questions about their goals and present them with alternatives, for many owners there is simply relief. Many of these owners have invested their lives in their businesses. There's no separation between home and office. It's an extension of their family. It's an extension of their life. And dealing with a liquidation can be devastating; for these entrepreneurs, it feels like a divorce or a death, even though they want to sell.

Rusty has a great phrase for our conversations with these owners: we want to encourage them to change gears, maybe even downshift a little. That's the recommendation we're making to you. After you pause and fully assess your options, selling to a third party may still make the most sense. But before you do, make sure that you haven't missed a better option.

Kelly's story is a good one because, for her, like many of the entrepreneurs with whom we work, her employees are like family members. These owners don't want the financial rewards of a sale to come while their employees are left in limbo. A new owner will be looking at metrics, but their decisions will impact lives and family members.

There are solutions like Kelly's, softer exits in which the owner maintains some ownership while releasing some equity and creating a path for the business to continue to meet the objectives that the original owners may have had at the business's inception. It's a path that supports the owners and their employees.

Could the Issue Actually Be You?

In this chapter we want to encourage you to pause and think about what you may have missed. We want your decision-making about your business to be fully informed with all possible options.

So we'll talk with you here as we would speak to you if we were sitting down face-to-face. And we'd start with this question:

Why?

Why are you at this point? Why are you considering exiting your business?

Take a moment and think about these questions. Don't answer too quickly. Consider the factors that have brought you to this point in your business's life cycle, and dig deep for the honest response.

Once you've considered the why, you should also spend time reflecting on the what. What are your goals for this transition? What matters to you? What does success look like for you when this transition is complete?

We like to say, "It all starts with a conversation," but frankly we want to spend much more time listening than talking. These are challenging questions, and we want you to have the time and space to answer them thoughtfully.

We want you to recognize the true value of your business, not just in the eyes of a potential buyer but in your eyes as well. What is your legacy—the one that you want to see continue? There is value not simply in the profit the business generates but also in the resources it provides to others and the relationships it has enabled.

We attend a lot of meetings with other entrepreneurs and business leaders, and one of the biggest benefits of getting a group of professionals together is that you can brainstorm and share solutions. Have you ever noticed how much easier it is to solve someone else's problems? Many professionals will quickly recommend that a fellow leader outsource a problem or hire a chief operating officer to manage financial challenges and yet fail to recognize that they should be doing exactly the same thing. That's why we encourage you to spend time identifying what has brought you to this point and what your objectives are for what's next.

There is value not simply in the profit the business generates but also in the resources it provides to others and the relationships it has enabled.

Many owners think a clean break is best because they're uncomfortable delegating. They've been extraordinarily successful, and they may not believe that anybody else can do it as well as they can. They have tried to delegate important roles but in the end always taken them back. They're reluctant to share the burdens of the business and think it might be uncomfortable retaining ownership of a company that someone else is running—perhaps a family member or a former employee or group of employees.

If this is where you are, we have an important message: it's okay to fail.

It's okay to allow a new CEO to take over and do things differently. It's okay to build a team around you and for that team to do a few things wrong. They'll learn, and they'll do things differently the next time, and the business will survive.

We understand that this can be challenging because we've had to navigate these transitions ourselves. But we've also experienced the satisfaction and, yes, pride in transitioning from boss to teacher/coach/advisor/co-owner.

BEFORE YOU SELL ...

Many business owners see only two options: running their business or selling their business. We urge them to identify the middle ground, guiding them to see that there are many possible strategies rather than one clear answer. We do this by coaching them through the four steps represented by this series of questions:

1. What is it that you don't like about running the business? What are your true goals for the future?

2. What do the numbers tell you? What are the economic rewards of continuing to own the business? What are the economic rewards of selling after paying expenses and taxes?

3. Do you understand your true cash flow? What is someone willing to pay today? What might they be willing to pay for a future stream of cash flow payments?

4. Which other options have you considered? Which alternatives best support your goals and objectives?

CHAPTER THREE:

YOU HAVE OPTIONS

When was the last time you took a sabbatical? We don't mean a vacation—one or even two weeks away from the physical office when you're still making calls, answering emails, popping into a Zoom meeting. We are talking about an extended leave from your daily work, a pause in which you can rest, recharge your batteries, maybe even assess (or reassess) your work horizon or retirement goals.

As we've spoken with more and more business owners who are ready and eager to sell, we've discovered that many of them were simply burned out. They were tired of juggling multiple roles, of having less time to do the work they actually enjoyed. It may have been years since they took extended time away from their business.

There's a reason why companies like Deloitte, General Mills, McDonald's, and Microsoft all have a sabbatical policy for employees. They've recognized that senior employees in leadership roles face enormous stress and can benefit from time away from the daily pressures and responsibilities of their work. They have found that those employees who take regular sabbaticals come back and have more significant impact on the organization, work longer, and experience more effective careers. This sabbatical also creates opportunities for others in the organization to step up and take on the responsibilities that they had not previously managed, ensuring continuity and a succession plan.

If you don't believe that anyone else in your organization can do what you do, perhaps they simply haven't had a chance to prove that they can. If you're feeling so tired that selling your business seems like the only way you'll have the time to enjoy life, you may not have tried other methods that we can bring to the table—methods like sabbaticals—to test the idea of selling before you actually sell.

> **If you don't believe that anyone else in your organization can do what you do, perhaps they simply haven't had a chance to prove that they can.**

In this chapter, we'll encourage you to pause and consider different solutions to the problems you've identified. Selling is always one option, but once you sell, the options are over. We can show you other options before you sell.

A Sale Reconsidered after Planning

Tim has a client story that demonstrates the importance of carefully planning and of identifying all options before proceeding with a sale. His client (we'll call him Matt) had a business that he had operated for many years, a business that provided a reasonable amount of income for Matt's family as the owners. Depending on the year, the true net spendable income ranged between $1 million and $2.5 million a year.

Matt came to Tim and asked for his help in selling the business. After studying the business's financials, Tim explained that they would likely only achieve five times that net income for the sale, given that Matt's business had not experienced much growth but was a consistent earner. Over the past five years, the business had averaged $2 million in adjusted EBITDA. As a result, Tim told Matt that his business was likely worth $10 million before taxes and expenses.

Matt was incredibly excited at the $10 million figure. But Tim asked him to pause and spend some time with Dave and Rusty on the planning side.

Because this was a family business and the family's expenses were integral to the decision-making, the team asked to involve the family in the discussion. This big-picture discussion involved dreams and aspirations as well as liabilities and expectations. The team learned that the family's basic expenses were around $300,000 a year, including taxes. The family's dream involved a capital expenditure for a winter home that would cost close to $2 million. They also wanted to maintain their current home—it was fully paid for but would cost roughly $35,000 a year to maintain. At the top of their wish list was helping their children and grandchildren on a regular basis. The family was extremely functional, but Matt's children had chosen professions that did not provide a higher level of income. Matt wanted to provide the maximum gifting each year to each of his three children and wanted to be responsible for the education expenses of each of the grandchildren. The family also wanted to be able to take at least two significant trips each year, one of which would be to the new winter home.

This is the kind of thoughtful planning that we encourage anyone thinking of selling a business to engage in. As you can see, once we engaged in a discussion that translated his wish list into dollars and cents, Matt recognized that he needed to rethink what had initially seemed like an exciting offer. He realized that his $10 million offer would result in proceeds of $6.5 million after taxes and expenses. He further realized that the income that could be earned on that $6.5 million, without taking significant amounts of risk, would be around $375,000 to $450,000 per year.

The challenge was that his wish list meant that his expenses would increase from $300,000 a year to include the gifting and traveling, plus the mortgage the family would need to take on the $2 million winter home. The new required earnings to support all the family's goals were close to $500,000 after taxes. In order for the family's portfolio to produce this much income, it would need to make 7.7 percent.

We spent time with Matt demonstrating what the odds were of a well-managed portfolio creating 7.7 percent return on a regular basis. We further showed him that the real risk to this strategy was a sharp drawdown in financial markets in the early years after selling, as this would severely damage the portfolio's ability to create even a 4 to 5 percent return, let alone a 7.7 percent return. Furthermore, we reminded him that he was not "in control" of this outcome like he had been in his business.

In the end, of course, the decision was Matt's. We explained that if he wanted to sell his company and live off the proceeds, it was possible but would require him to sharply reduce his withdrawals during difficult periods. We showed him a model in which he reduced his expenses from his planned $500,000 a year to $250,000 in those difficult years; in that scenario he would maintain his principal based on historical market results. We advised on how to reduce these expenses accordingly by eliminating things like travel.

Then we showed Matt an alternative, one that was very radical, given that his intent was to sell his business. We noted that there had never been a time in his business when it had not produced at least $1 million of income. We suggested that if we eliminated his salary and benefits, there had never been a time when it hadn't produced $1.2 million in income. The point that we wanted to make was that this was at least 100 percent above Matt's required spending to fulfill everything on his wish list, including the gifting and the second home, not to mention taxes and spending.

His response? "That's great, but I don't want to keep operating the business. I don't want to have all the risks of being a business owner."

This is certainly a valid consideration and one that helped us better identify a motivator for his decision to sell.

The next step in the planning process was to look at how we could solve both of these concerns—operating the business and assuming all risk—without simply selling the business and advising Matt to reduce his spending during difficult years. Step one was to look at the risk question. Here, we worked with one of our property and casualty specialists to assess how best to reduce risk on product liability claims as well as personal liability. We also made sure that all debts and pledges that could have any personal liability or guarantees were removed.

Next, we addressed the concern that he no longer wanted to continue to operate the business. We spent time with him assessing how and where he spent his time at the company. He ultimately recognized that he had two major roles in the organization. First, he was the primary manager of the financial side of the business. He wasn't writing the checks, but he was reviewing the work of the accounting and business management staff and setting budgets, capital expenditure requirements, etc. Second, he was the visionary who identified the direction for the business.

As we spoke with him, we realized that this second role was the one he actually enjoyed. He just didn't like the business management, HR, and accounting responsibilities.

We told Matt that there was a different option for him to consider. He could find a chief financial officer who could manage the business functions and promote one of his top marketing executives to the role of president to represent the company when needed. He could then remain as the visionary—the role he still loved.

Matt's initial response was "It's not that simple." But as we continued our discussions, as he reflected, he realized that it actually *was* that simple. What we helped him realize was that there were qualified candidates who could become the CFO; he already had an internal candidate to fill the leadership role. Instead of selling his company, he had an alternative. He could keep the company, delegate all but the visionary role, and withdraw $1 million worth of dividends a year.

Several years later Matt came to us with a big box filled with our favorite scotches and wines as a thank-you gift. He told us that our planning process had saved him nearly $4 million. More importantly it had created the lifestyle that he had dreamed of—a second home, the ability to support his children and grandchildren.

"It's hard to teach an old dog new tricks," he told us, "but that's just what you did."

The Magic Wand

Planning is critical, both to clarify your goals and to identify your alternatives. Dave instructs his clients to pick up their magic wand, wave it, and then describe what their "perfect world" looks like if they proceed with their decision to sell. Are they selling the company and stepping away completely? Are they selling it as an employee stock ownership plan (ESOP) so that a group of internal employees will buy the business while the client retains some ownership or even control? Is it a complete sale or a partial sale?

We want owners to paint this complete picture of their perfect world to make sure that it lines up with the reality. Most business owners have dedicated much of their life to building that business; they've either grown it themselves or steered its direction for a long time. They care about the employees who are currently there; they look at them as family. Their name has been on the door, and their self-worth has been connected to that business for a significant period.

When we begin to discuss a potential sale, the focus for the owner is principally on the economics of the deal, the financial worth that they can extract from a negotiation. But as we continue these conversations, as we invite them to describe what their "magic wand" has revealed, what starts to surface are the emotional ties and the important facets that have nothing to do with dollars and cents.

It's also interesting to engage them in questions of who might fill the roles they have been filling. These owners have coached and mentored their senior team over the years. They know who has their kind of focus, who has the skills to step up and assume responsibility for selling, for financial oversight, for representing the company in public settings. They also know when they don't have the right people internally and which roles might require an external hire.

In the story we shared at the start of this chapter, we noted the importance of engaging the family in this "perfect world" visualization. For many of the owners we work with, they've kept business goals and family goals separate. But what we've discovered, as we guide owners and their families through these discussions, is that personal and professional goals often intersect at this stage.

It's equally important to engage in these discussions when there is potential disagreement or conflict over next steps. Sometimes the identity of the matriarch or the patriarch and the extended family is the business.

It's critical to understand that and to create an action plan that ensures that the transition of the business doesn't impair that identity that has been shaped by decades of work and focus. These are likely not people who will just retire and be happy. They will want, even need, ongoing roles in the company or some other pursuit. Identifying that now, before a sale, can keep families from making terrible mistakes that will cause problems within the family for decades to come.

We've worked with several different companies in various industries in what we call the "shirtsleeves to shirtsleeves in three generations" scenario. These are businesses where, by the third generation, there's tremendous dissent about how best to proceed. They are asking questions about whether to grow the business, sell the business, or identify a different niche in the industry. It may be that the business was started by an entrepreneur, inherited and run by her children (siblings), and then the third generation may be siblings, cousins, even in-laws. You need to be able to navigate through conversations that almost invariably come from running a family business when the family can't agree on where their focus should be or on what's important to them. These can create land mines that ripple through the family in a very negative way.

When you're in the midst of those conversations, you can feel the emotion move through the room. But our message to all clients is the same. We ask all involved parties what their perfect world is. We ask about goals and expectations. And then we identify alternatives, options that will hopefully create a path for reconciliation or at least a smoothing over of the waters that can allow families to move forward. We don't do this by ourselves. We create a team by identifying tax professionals, insurance professionals, and sources of expert legal advice as any deals are finalized as well as encouraging our clients to work with a family therapist to address any deep-seated issues that may be impacting their ability to reach a consensus.

In these kinds of situations, we tell our clients, "You want to be able to sit around the Thanksgiving table and feel good about being shoulder to shoulder with each other." Our goal is to identify a solution that everyone feels comfortable with, one that facilitates that enjoyable Thanksgiving dinner.

No "Right" Answer

We spend more time listening than talking as we work with clients in this "discovery" stage. We each do this a bit differently. Dave uses a structured set of cards. These serve as a tool designed to elicit answers to questions he asks family unit by family unit, owner by owner. These are often questions not directly related to the business, things like "How do you feel about charitable giving?" and "How do you feel about caring for your children or aging parents?" Rusty uses a traditional yellow legal pad instead of a set of cards, and Tim likes to ask these questions over drinks or lunch in a relaxed setting. The tools may be different, but the goals are the same. We want our clients to tell us their story and identify what's important in their world.

Too often, business owners assume that there are only two options: run the business themselves or sell the business. Our purpose in the discovery stage is to identify other options, and there are many more than we could possibly discuss in this short book. What we share with most owners is that there are multiple strategies they can pursue rather than one clear answer. Through planning, they can identify which strategy makes the most sense for them, their family, and their business.

This depends on us being very clear about the owner's goals. Too often, business brokers and investment bankers skip this step and just go straight to "Let's sell." That can become one of the biggest mistakes a business owner will ever make, and it comes from a professional with a conflict—they only get paid if you sell. In this book we encourage you to not simply hire a professional in business transition but to also hire one with planning expertise first and foremost.

The result of these question-and-answer sessions may be a solution in which you solve for what you don't like and keep what you do. There are options in which you source a talent solution instead of a sales solution by replacing yourself, or consider recapping the equity in your company to create the liquidity you need, or create a transition of ownership with key employees.

It's important to do your due diligence and recognize the economics of keeping the business versus selling to understand your cash flow and identify your true goals for the future. These are all critical to the planning process.

But there's also the X factor, and we encourage our clients to assess this as they consider options. There may be more than economic rewards for keeping your business; there may be emotional rewards as well. You may welcome the opportunity to transition into a new role of educator, mentor, visionary, or even spiritual leader. You may want to create an opportunity to stay in an industry where you have the most value.

And sometimes, if after all this planning you're still ready to sell, it may be helpful to pause and think about who you would like to buy your business. You may want to sell to senior management or to an individual or group in the company. Often the biggest obstacle is that these individuals or this group are enthusiastic but simply lack the financial resources to do so. There are strategies that owners can use to sell a portion

It's important to do your due diligence and recognize the economics of keeping the business versus selling to understand your cash flow and identify your true goals for the future.

of the business, retain a portion of the business, and gradually sell the remaining shares over time (such as the ESOP or perhaps through taking back a note from the buyers, as we referenced earlier).

Minority recap is another option we explore with clients. If their goal is to access a significant amount of cash for a second home, or something else that is high on their wish list, a minority recap is a strategy that enables them to access cash without waiting for the business to sell. It affords the company the opportunity to go to a lender and replace some of what is currently equity on the company's balance sheet with debt. For example, you might want to access $10 million, and you own a company producing $5 million in EBITDA; with a minority recap, you can get $10 million out of the equity part of the business and replace it with $10 million of debt on your company's balance sheet. The interest on $10 million will not change the ability for your company to continue to operate profitably.

This recapitalization approach does not typically impugn the balance sheet to the point that it would not look attractive to a future buyer. It's literally a way to pull some equity out of the business or to bring in a buyer for a part of your equity (usually a closely held or internal buyer) with small amounts of debt that the business can then service without impairing its operations.

Another option we encourage certain clients to consider is the use of their company stock in a charitable gifting plan. If our client has expressed charitable intentions as part of their wish list, a potential gift could be structured so that a charitable entity is involved in part of a larger stock sale transaction and can help defray or mitigate some of the capital gains taxes going forward. An owner who is nearing retirement might choose to gift their shares in the company to a nonprofit with an immediate put option in them, meaning the nonprofit has to sell the shares back to the company right away. This enables the owner (the stock-holder) to use charitable gifting but to do it in a way that doesn't damage the company's ownership structure.

What we want owners to recognize is that there is not one "right" answer to the question of whether or not they should sell their business. There are multiple strategies that can best be identified by thoughtful planning and by taking the time to answer key questions and identify your goals. One of our favorite clients decided that he wanted to do more for charity. We analyzed charitable gift structures as a way for him to sell his company and defray taxes. In the end the company was so profitable that after the sale, the income from investments could not replace the cash flow from the company. The client didn't just want to give all his funds away; he wanted to use the income on funds to benefit charity now versus after his death or much later. His company was structured in a way that we could take advantage of a relatively unique idea. We took the ground and building on which the company was located (which was owned by the client), separated these from the company, and gave the real estate to a charity. We then had the client sign a long-term lease with the charity, and this created income that the client was really giving away to charity at a much more significant level than before but without giving up control of the income-generating business.

Too many owners spend all their time on planning for their business's next year or five years and none on their own exit strategy. We want to encourage you to prepare now for what that exit will involve and how you can make sure that it supports your goals and expectations.

CHAPTER FOUR:

WHEN SELLING IS THE RIGHT DECISION

As we've discussed it's always best to begin early to plan for your exit strategy. That preparation and planning should be thoughtful and deliberate. We recognize that years of preparation aren't always possible, but planning is a must. Sometimes, after we've worked with clients to identify their goals and discuss their motivations and expectations, we determine that it is the right time for them to sell their business. When that happens, it's important to continue to implement the five Ps: proper planning prevents poor processes.

First, let's look at one example of when that planning revealed that selling was the right decision.

Sale and Lease

A client of ours, we'll call her Marla, was a young entrepreneur working with partners to operate a successful business. That business produced $2 million of net income per year; each time they opened a new location, the income increased by roughly $500,000 per year, but it cost nearly $2 million to open a new location. Marla's partners, who were not active in the business, were unwilling to fund future growth. Marla came to us as business management consultants and asked what she should do.

After spending time with her reviewing her business and the challenges she had encountered, we told her that she had a dysfunctional partnership. We recommended that she take her equity out of the business and start anew without the constraints of partners who did not support her growth. We demonstrated our reasoning by showing her what her equity could grow to if the business could continue to expand versus what would happen if she stayed in her current position without any additional growth. Marla was worried that her partners would prevent her from continuing to work in the industry if she left or sold the company. She documented this in a way that prompted us to dive a bit deeper.

Marla's company was in a fairly hot industry; it would not be hard to find buyers for the company. Her industry required that the properties she operated have certain restrictive zoning. As we investigated further, we recognized that it was very difficult to find new locations with this kind of zoning, which was why there was interest in acquiring companies like Marla's. The standard offer in the market was a very generous multiple on EBITDA. However, regardless of how high we could get the multiple, the company was still only making $2 million a year. After we adjusted for things like Marla's benefits and salary, we were only at $2.25 million. If we sold the company, we could do so for about seven times this or $15.75 million before expenses and taxes.

However, we also learned something else. Acquiring companies were willing to pay rental income for properties like Marla's in the range of $50,000 to $75,000 per month or $600,000 to $900,000 per year.

It was time for a conversation with Marla. We explained that what looked like a very attractive offer of $15.75 million was actually half of that after federal and state taxes. The net result, $7.8 million, when invested at 5 percent return, would produce around $380,000 of income per year.

We recommended that she invite her partners to meet with us, and in that gathering, we explained that Marla had identified a better solution than to continue to operate the business, one that would alleviate the risks and uncertainties that all businesses face. We suggested that they sell the company for a reduced exit price but demand a long-term lease on the property that was triple net so that Marla and her partners would have no exposure to ongoing expenses. (In a triple-net lease, the tenant assumes all expenses for the property.) We helped identify a AAA-rated tenant. The net result was that Marla and her partners received $12.5 million in the sale but also held a thirty-year lease from a *Fortune* 500 company at $900,000 a year.

As part of the negotiation of the sale, Marla requested that the buyer release her from any noncompete moving forward. Today, she operates a business in the same industry that is six times the size of her previous business, and she is still receiving her share of the rental income. She used her share of the sale proceeds as the capital to launch her new business.

The Buyers

As Marla's story illustrates, the strategic planning we're recommending extends to a thoughtful assessment of who the best buyer should be if selling is the right option. It's not simply a matter of who is prepared to offer the highest figure.

The *synergistic buyer* has a specific interest in a company, often because they are operating in the same space. They're looking for rapid and long-term growth and want to use the sale to leverage existing structures. They may be using the sale to buy a product and a customer list. They are generally less interested in a company's people and its infrastructure because they usually already have people and infrastructure in place.

The second kind of buyer is a *financial buyer*. This buyer is really an investor; they are usually not operating in the same industry but instead are interested in strong investment opportunities. In some cases these buyers may be private equity buyers. These are buyers with money that they want to invest.

The *participant buyer* is the third type of buyer. The participant buyer is someone who likely is in the same industry or an adjacent industry. They may have sold their company, took some time away from business, and now are ready to get back into the game. They also may be a senior manager at a major company but don't see an opportunity to advance further in their current organization. They are businesspeople who want to make an investment in a company they intend to actively run themselves. Unlike the synergistic buyer, they don't have a preexisting business into which the new acquisition will be merged. These buyers typically have 10 or 20 percent of the purchase price in cash, and they've met with a lender and been preapproved on financing for a specific amount of the purchase price.

The *internal buyer* is the fourth category of buyer. These are people who already work at the company. They may not know that the company is for sale, but if they knew, they would be interested in becoming the next owner. We've spent time in previous chapters talking a bit about how this can be a great option for an owner, but the reality is that these internal buyers rarely make themselves known ahead of time. We have to identify them and create a way for them to have the resources to purchase the company, working with them to identify financing options that make sense for them and for the seller.

Most business brokers use a shotgun approach when identifying a buyer for a company. They create a fancy book of data and send it out to hundreds, if not thousands, of potential buyers to see who responds. They take pride in their ability to access such a huge database.

Our belief is that there is a better way. We use our client's goals to identify three to five top candidates. These candidates are specifically the kind of buyers who will enable our client to achieve the goals they identified. We then approach those potential buyers directly. It is our belief that if we can't get a reasonable offer with one of them, there is no reason to pursue hundreds of others and have everyone in the client's industry know that they are for sale!

We recently worked with a client whose industry had a lot of transactions going on in it. We saw big consolidators. Private equity had come into the industry and was backing people to buy other companies as a source of growth. That meant that there were both synergistic buyers and financial buyers for our client's business. The prices that were being paid for businesses in our client's industry eliminated the possibility of a participant buyer or an internal buyer being able to match the offers. Here is an example where a wider net would make sense, as there is competitive bidding. In this case we found several companies whose interests and goals aligned with those of our client and identified the best matches for our client's company.

The Process

At the end of the day, our focus is on making sure that our clients are fully prepared, fully informed, and absolutely clear on how and why selling is the best choice to achieve their short-term and long-term goals. We want them to look beyond the sale price to all the implications, both personal and financial. It may be a detailed assessment of tax strategy. It may be a gentle reminder that the health insurance and even the life insurance they currently have through the company will change dramatically. It may mean that family or current key employees may no longer be involved.

We've discussed the key first steps of our process—identifying post-sales goals and considering potential types of buyers. Next, we work to tell the story of the company to potential buyers using the sellers' value statements to clarify why this business is so valuable. We encourage owners to narrow their focus here. You don't want to discuss every facet of the business; instead, what are the three or four really valuable things about the company? That's where the presentation should be centered. The value statement is what will matter most to the buyer at the end of the day; we want to help build it so that the buyer doesn't have to build it themselves.

Tim calls this process "selling blue sky." It's highlighting the ways in which this acquisition is a clear win for the buyer. You might highlight the fact that the infrastructure is 100 percent in place or that the company is already one of the top three players in a different market, so it will be easy to expand the concept with the right management and capital in place. The technology, the people, the capabilities are all ready to go—a much better deal than having to build a company from scratch. We also help our clients restate their financials, removing owner expenses and any other one-time expenses. We break out the sales by customer to alleviate the fear that any one customer leaving is a risk, show the longevity of the employees through the creation of employment agreements, and break out expenses by category so the buyer can understand them more clearly and feel that there is full transparency, thereby increasing trust. We graph sales by region or sector and show what the size of each product's market is and where the company stands in the industry so as to allow the buyer to be able to visualize that there is plenty of room for growth. Finally, we identify weaknesses so the buyer can see themselves as a solution to any problems.

Next, we do the same thing most bankers or brokers do: we identify key people in the organization who the buyer should meet when the time is right and bring them into the process, such as the CFO. We create a prospective buyer list and review it for any potential conflicts with the seller. We create a blind—a document for potential buyers that lists the industry, the sales numbers, and other basic information to determine a buyer's interest without revealing the company's (our client's) name. When a buyer responds to our inquiry, we ensure that buyers are able to close, have them sign a nondisclosure agreement, and then begin discussions designed to find the buyer who will be the best fit.

A key piece of advice we give to our clients, one that we hope has been highlighted in this book, is this should never be a one-size-fits-all process. Each business is unique; it deserves a thoughtful, curated approach to ensure that decisions are made correctly and in a way that supports the business and the owner. That's why it's critical to *never negotiate your own deal*. After nearly three decades of working with clients, we can tell you that the sophistication that exists in professional buyers offers them a real advantage over most sellers. Understanding the market, the different structures that different types of buyers use, and the available financing vehicles is critical to maximizing the value of any deal.

Michael Lewis has a famous quote: "Those who say don't know, those who know don't say." Such is the case in maximizing the value for our clients. Experience really matters here. Our experience does not come simply from working with clients. Like most things we do, our experience comes from real life. From owning businesses ourselves, from meeting payrolls, from solving expense problems, and from selling those businesses for ourselves. We think this is the real value statement for our clients because we really believe that we understand the market for selling businesses and, perhaps more importantly, why they should not be sold.

Yes, you will ultimately need to consult a lawyer, a tax professional, perhaps even a risk analyst. But before you spend your hard-earned money on fees, work with an expert

Understanding the market, the different structures that different types of buyers use, and the available financing vehicles is critical to maximizing the value of any deal.

in not just selling a business but also in planning succession strategy to make sure that the sale is the right option. Allow that expert to get the deal negotiated, to find the right price and, of course, the right buyer. Don't start writing six-figure checks to the CPA or the lawyer and especially an investment banker on day one. And remember the five *P*s: proper planning prevents poor processes.

CONCLUSION

There's so much more we'd like to share with you, but in a book this size, we have to focus on a few key points. So we'll end with this encouragement: if you are a business owner, and you think you're ready to sell, slow down. Slow down and go back through the planning process. Slow down and think through your answers to key questions. Why are you ready to sell? What are your expectations for yourself, your family, the business you're selling? What are your goals? Which next steps will ensure that you can meet those expectations and goals?

You've invested so much time in your business that it's important to invest time in understanding how best to transition to what's next. Your business has had a major impact on you, your family, your employees, your vendors, your customers. Don't skip to the end without considering all the options available to you that will affect all of them! The only way to do that is to go through the planning process.

Our recommendation is to plan for your exit strategy early and revisit those plans periodically as your plans change, your business grows or expands, and your goals evolve. Think about which steps will best support your expenses and your aspirations.

We said it at the beginning: it starts with a conversation. We'd like to continue the conversation we've started with this book. We'd welcome the opportunity to meet with you, discuss your transition plan, and help you create solutions to meet your business challenges and identify the best future actions for you and your business.

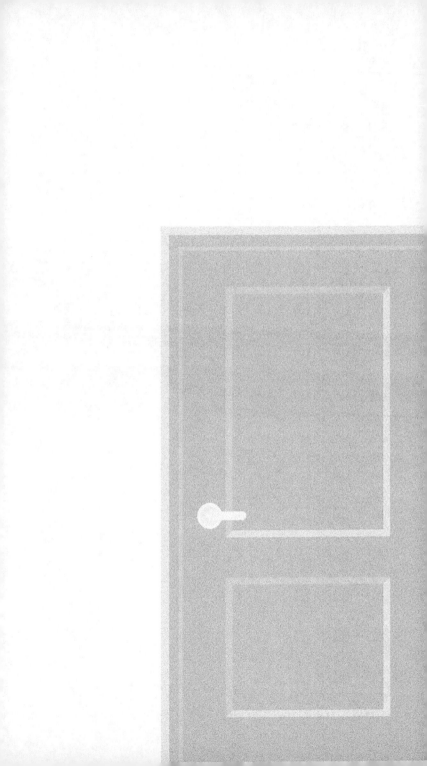

WHAT MAKES US DIFFERENT

The business consulting and succession planning industry standard is commission based, charging a percentage of the transactional value. This can range as high as 9 percent for some deals that are very small. On average a $20 million transaction would be about 6 percent, while a $50 million transaction would be about 4 percent. The industry would call these success fees, but they are really just commissions. In addition, most people in the industry charge an up-front fee that can be as small as $20,000 and as high as $100,000 to pay for their time before the company is listed for sale.

As we talk about throughout the book, we are planners first. That by itself makes us very different because we do not begin the process with the idea of convincing the client to sell their business. In fact, in many cases, a client will come to us thinking they are going to sell their business, and we end up finding a superior solution to accomplish their goals in other ways.

Since we are planners first, we charge a flat fee per year to our clients based on the amount of work that we are doing. This flat fee covers not only the work that we're doing for the client in business transition services but also all our planning work, liquid investment work, retirement plan work, estate and tax management work, and P&C/other insurance management work, as well as managing the other professionals around the client, such as accountants and lawyers.

Let's consider a client who is selling a business for $40 million. The industry is pricing that at 5 percent to make the math easy. The commissions on that sale would be $2 million. This would not include any of the previously mentioned services beyond helping to sell the business. In our structure, most importantly, the client is not being led down a path that has only one solution, which would be selling the company.

You may be asking, "Don't you still need a broker or a banker?" In practice, we would tell you that, for those businesses that are correctly positioned for sale versus one of the other solutions that we might bring to the table, we more often than not find there is a limited number of ideal candidates to purchase that business. If there are five or ten candidates, it is silly to pay a broker $2 million to make the phone calls we can easily make. If, however, the client has a business that should be marketed to the masses, we will act as a fiduciary and go out and find the right broker to list that company for the client. However, in our real-life experience, we can negotiate those commissions down by at least half because we have already done all the work for the broker. All the broker is really doing is sending out the book that we created to that broker's prospective list of buyers. Even in this rare case, the client would still end up saving a great deal of money.

If you'd like to know more about Private Wealth Asset Management and the services we provide to businesses like yours, feel free to reach out by phone at *888-644-PWAM*, or visit our website at *privatewealth.com*.

Value Statement

Private Wealth Asset Management
brings financial peace of mind by surrounding
clients with a team of experts who know them
personally and who manage all their financial
matters. Our advisors are supported by a team
of specialists who are subject matter experts,
all right at home in your local market! We bring
expertise and deliver objectivity, transparency
and choice to you and your family. Our
commitment is to assemble the right team of
professionals to deliver the exceptional service
our clients deserve.

private wealth
ASSET MANAGEMENT

9 781642 254068